Exile in My Homeland

by

Dale Jacobson

1663 Liberty Drive, Suite 200
Bloomington, Indiana 47403
(800) 839-8640
www.AuthorHouse.com

© 2005 Dale Jacobson. All Rights Reserved.

No part of this book may be reproduced, stored in a retrieval system, or transmitted by any means without the written permission of the author.

First published by AuthorHouse 08/08/05

ISBN: 1-4208-6120-4 (sc)

Printed in the United States of America
Bloomington, Indiana

This book is printed on acid-free paper.

Acknowledgments:

A substantial portion of this poem has been published by *Island Hills Online Chapbooks*, edited by the poet Gary David. The section for Rachel Corrie was published in a slightly different version by the online journal, *The Pedestal Magazine*.

The back cover photograph was taken by the lovely and beautiful painter Therese Olejniczak. I also want to acknowledge her advice and help in the design of the front and back covers. The front cover photograph was taken by myself.

Such a process, in which thought (i.e., the response of memory) and the general environment are indissolubly linked, is evidently of the nature of a cycle (though this cycle should be regarded more accurately as always opening out into a spiral). This cyclical (or spiral) movement, in which thought has its full actual and concrete existence, includes also communication of thoughts between people (who are parts of each other's environment) and it goes indefinitely far into the past. Thus, at no stage can we properly say that the *overall process* of thought begins or ends. Rather, it has to be seen as one unbroken totality of movement, not belonging to any particular person, place, time, or group of peoples.

–David Bohm

The Spectre is the Reasoning Power in Man; & when separated
From Imagination, and closing itself as in steel, in a Ratio
Of the Things of Memory. It thence frames Laws and Moralities
To destroy Imagination! the Divine Body, by Martyrdoms & Wars

–William Blake

But you have dishonored the poor man. Is it not the rich who oppress you, is it not they who drag you into court?

–James 2: 6

I

1.

When those great deep shoulders of granite shift
the foundations of cities shudder and the moon
whitens like cold fire on the ancient petroglyphs,
freezes the first graffiti of the continent in millennial time.

The wind sings a narrative of erosions and erased camps–
hunts a lost note of jars among shards of clay,
urns that once held water like a circular meditation...

and summers rush back to me like bullets of light
that shatter into constellations– all days consumed
by the night that kneels over sleepers,
collecting dreams like water in its big dipper.

Night that cradles the earth a bright robin egg
or future skull whose eyes are lost in the dark,
night of subterrestrial waters with their cool passages,
night transparent to itself, darkness leaning perpetually
into darkness,
                original cipher that dreamed the universe...

Those young days.
                Torn away by each evening
descending,
          the moon scaling its cold vigil over the ruins
of gone peoples. I came to my continent companioned
by my shadow whose hand always touched the earth,
the earth shifting,
the light shifting,
all shadows lengthening
                toward night where primroses
darken...
      and collect in their dark circles
the silences of mouths that sang each day bright.

2.

My native land...
          In my childhood days
when everything turned in waves of light
and the sun singing cicada stretched
a taut wire across summer afternoon,
an electric meditation the frequency of Zen,
the world was home to my wandering,
gravel roads, green shuddering fields,
meandering river that kept its own time.

No earth beyond the prairie
leaning into the horizon, falling toward

a mirage of distance, far memory of itself,
I felt all its stored time beneath my feet:
buried seasons and centuries, the elder
energy of creatures that had entered rock
pillowed on the long slide of the geological dark.

Earth near and far,
              at my feet long lands
of a child's eye,
              horizon always a step
away and rolling toward the crisp and deep
sounds of dusk:
              crickets, doors, voices,
lone dogs calling from the center of time–
and then night came on,
lunar shadows shuffling their ghosts,
the great trees swaying in the dark wind.

The land, razed and rolled by glaciers,
made wealthy by rain and sun,
held its lakes and silence, rivers and fields,
like a mind in the center of dreaming,
summer, bright jewel of the year:
the sun shimmering in the tassels of corn,
this harsh prairie mother in whose other eye
autumn raged blazing death and winter stormed.

I saw the wings of hawks flattened in the dust,
barns collapsing upon their emptiness
in slow motion through the century– everything

crushed–
pulled to earth, worn down under
the open naked depth of sky
even as new waters rippled and roiled each spring–
my great uncle in his casket more deaf than usual,
all his years blank on the cool mask of a face–
people, animals, houses and nests fell apart,
and the winds tore down what they weakened.

The soul of the prairie–
golden rod and blue flag insignia,
immense– I took for my own–
greater than the towns and church steeples–
greater than my nation, its tired century–
this land whose son I am.

3.

I later learned others came before,
whom I imagined haunting the trails
we roamed by the river, who once
wandered where I did in those young
tall days, spirits out of time I came to know
as I knew the land–
               far peoples
whose footsteps once imprinted the soil,
whose voices reached into the wind
like ours calling each other's names,
and though the wind had made them

anonymous, and though I was told
my forebears came from across an ocean,
they were my ancestors just as the stones
were old, and I felt their presence
in the habits of the prairie, the trees
that rumored into the dusk,
the turning cool light, deadfall hours
under the pale soaring moon,
and their time I felt deep in the earth.

4.

My footsteps followed theirs, a legacy...
and walked beyond (each morning a frontier,
each day collected by dusk moths,
and the night haunted by lost worlds).

Though their lives were nowhere written,
their names taken flight,
                          their footsteps
so faint not even the wind could stalk them,
in my mornings I felt their morning near
as I felt the earth ancient–
                    ancestors
born under my same sun and moon,
stars whose threads of light
                          touch the tips of trees,
like myself born to the same mantle of dusk
and cloak of dreams on the edge of the world

where black furies and fires and fears burn
the remnants of day in the orange hour–

all of us born to the vagrant winds never the same.

                5.

I wandered the country–
                how many
summers ago now folded away like faded letters?–
the winding river,
                the redwing blackbirds
flitting in the ditches and the wide fields,
in childhood driven from town by voices,
harsh, loud, they rose up like looming snakes
spitting caustic words,
                ashes...

The adults were angry.
                And beneath their anger,
the bitter quiet of injured souls
who had lost their place,
                worn down,
beaten down,
         worn out,
                down and out...
their lives used up on work, the secret war,
(and older wars they inherited, childhood
wounds turned inward, the gifts of parents)

and the other war a conflagration...

They retreated into themselves,
my parents:
         my mother like a raccoon
addicted to glossy objects and baubles,
anything that shined against the dark,
small weapons against loneliness, her parents
too poor to notice more than survival–

and my father's gentleness ripped from him
by his Baptist mother whose God was more selfish
than that phony artist who demolished Europe.
They wanted a tool,
         a word to halt the wind,
but their rages never found the charmed calm.

The wind was history
         and older than history,
it came from somewhere hollow, turning
on absence, making its own road,
born from a dead tree gathering emptiness
or the long faded notes of a Neanderthal flute
carved from the shin bone of a bear...
time falling into time...
         lost music...
                   yesterday
a corridor out of the past, train of ghosts,
hospital for the dead,
         a long discontent...

Always departing, it spoke of departures–
the poverties they feared,
                "the poor house"
my father kept mentioning, whose address
I could never find though I hunted
all over town among the poorer houses
and even places it might be hidden in shame,
curious about the house we might move into.

It was gravity they feared, the old griefs,
The Great Depression,
           a century at war–
                      history.

And in autumn the wind came dragging its feet
with the rasping dance of dry leaves...

They wanted to stop time long enough to locate
themselves–
      or their lost childhood–
                our parents
nightly painted into the dark by their own shadows...
and then the new world rose each dawn
with a strange light and they wondered:
"Is this the country we built from our dreams?
Are these our children?"

Beyond the city I sought the voices quieted,

hard words that traveled the edges of pain—
and those I heard at school, bully critiques,
cowardly cliques learning to hate need,
the call of the past, in themselves and others—

Beyond the playground and the great class project
I wanted to hear the world,
      the place of belonging
I once knew—
   and my own voice calmed among
the simpler clans more in sync,
     small animals
rustling and scurrying their clandestine affairs
with the sound of arranging paper in the leaves,
birds building their own space by wing or song,
opening airy hallways by warble and call,
and the always present river rippling its way
past the solemn stones,
     the verb and noun married.

In the center of everything the quiet,
the high balance of noon tilting west,
dusk sliding between the light,
the private and public stillness inside the cooling air,
the huge hollowness of atoms
       secretly singing,
the universe a drop of creation falling
or not falling
    within the shaft of a well with no wall—
falling nowhere—

       floating:

              the irreducible moment:

the stirring branches within the void,

beneath song the pure pause that is silence:

wind,
        origin...

leaves turning toward the night–

everything
        one belonging,

the sharp cry out of the beginning of time.

II

1.

It was a world ancient powers cast up,
those early days when everything
seemed eternal–
                and all names
were mighty and rang like creation.

And each day was lifted from
the roiling sheen of an infinite coin
struck by moon glow in the wishing well
of dream waters–
                where quantum fire
sang in voices too high to hear–
and shimmering images came and went
and became day again–
                  from the depths
of sleep each dawn was flung up
and swift wings invented the horizons!

And then,
        when the only coin I had to spend
against all the real estate of the world
was myself,

        play made the day great!–
(in the bliss of my ignorance of war).

All the world depended upon knowing
someone within myself was known–
the wide prairie light flowed home
when my name was given back:
and I went
        out
             into the day,
                   transporting
the lonesome spaces of my body
night had opened and emptied–
                   and in sharing
and being shared the deep voices within myself
sang free...
        My fellow tribe of children
without king or khan, high priest or chief,
created the small legend of ourselves,
                   original
communion without ritual before religion
made us kneel down to original sin–

And in evening our voices floated out
in the coolness of a world dissolving,
in the weaving energy of our wild running
our calls grew large across the void...

And then in the heavy dark of time silence
reigned until the rude crows glossy

with the polish of midnight pulled from
the moon's shadows the colors of dawn–
and once again the sharp cries of jays
like diamond knives shattered midair
and clouds moved across their blue unfenced
acres,
      across my summers massive barges laden
with dark vapors,
             waters that had climbed
from the ocean on ladders thin as light–
or were hauled up by the vagrant wind
that touches everything like an afterthought,
the workings of the day
                immense without effort!

Weather seems easy and is always free...
and perhaps governed by the secret everyone
yearns,
      open as the mutable sky.

"Energy is eternal delight," the great Blake said.

And yet,
      a hard thought to hold when
you're under it and its bad,
              bad yen
the forecast,
      the sky falling.

In the land of play all was not serene!

I learned the world could change–
                              the day
darken,
        the clouds marshal a black force,
the prairie build danger out of distance.

And when the summer storms broke
and lightning cast its signatures like ice
cracking,
          fissures cascading in the darkening chasm,
and thunder's burden of silence collapsed
through all the hollowness of the ages,
its accumulated rumblings shaking
the foundations of the sky,
                            and the winds
gathered out of nowhere as if the gates
of a riotous congregation of ghosts had opened,
weaving huge empty baskets,
                            the wombs
of tornadoes,
              effortless transmutation–
                                        I remember
the world revealed its indifferent face: *power*
surged and swept where power would–
the heavens shifted,
                    the winds whipped the tall
grasses in the wild ditches,
                            the trees flailed the air:

and then I saw the smallness of my hands...

2.

I came to learn, as we all must who lose
everything at last,
        how nothing lasts
in a world where the weather can tear down
your house,
        and even the people who make
the house large,
        and even closer to home,
the house I lasted in–
        my life–
           and then
where would I go,
        where could anyone go
broken like a toy–
        outlasted by the world,
become forever late,
        always the last one
home,
    become a memory, a space
in someone else's day–
        become so lost
not even a trace of my shadow could be found
except roaming dim along the dark margin
of moonlight in the dreams of others?

I didn't understand this method, though
some deep voice in my solitude said
it had to be: change,
     transilience,
         energy dance,
happenstance,
    a world built on ruin–
          inbuilt
corruption:
   myself changing–
       youth
so hard to let go because it is all we know...
place we begin,
   holy origins...

But the world knows more,
        mandates
metamorphosis...
    (Does the butterfly know
the sleeping colors within its cocoon?)

The world shifts and the wind shuffles fate...

And I grew taller,
    older,
       Jack of the bean stalk
stalking my giant,
    who was myself–
changed by the simple act of breathing,
learning another world even as

I didn't notice the vanishing shores
the past growing deeper into gray
horizons floating islands of failing light
far off–
        somehow those days drifted away
their roads fields bright flowers people
voices ghosts of memory unreachable
hands haunting the edges of the only
country I knew, itself becoming history–

my interior worlds and words...
                            the needs of the past...

3.

I entered the sacred shade,
on the way home from school
when I was seven: immense
evergreens–
        I walked the turning path
that dipped and climbed through the grove
of spruce where late afternoon light
filtered into a room of looming guardians,
giants–
        place secluded like a vault,
a sanctuary where all the voices of the wind
gathered in those great swaying branches...

Trees burst into flame,
planes sweep low, birds scream
like voices escaping nightmare–
napalm furrows the forest into smoke!
Heat waves roll up the sky!

I saw ten years later a country
torn apart, land scorched and scarred,
I saw on t.v. the jets like whips
slash the land–
              at seventeen
almost draft age,
                  eligible to die
in a place on t.v.–
                  I saw Viet Nam
a country somewhere beyond
all the hills I knew where
my schoolmates went to go
crazy and never come home,
and my country I loved I never
found again,
           the war exiled
everyone the wide prairie,
open roads
          the world became
a tomb of the living the dead
where whole forests and cities
were smoke locked in a box.

Bad yen the forecast–
                    napalm,
                              the sky
falling,
         advancing shelves of fire
consume the forest,
                    and I am there,
or could be if the presence I call myself
were born in another country–
                              I am
in my home land a Viet Cong, Charlie,
gook,
      who once entered a sacred shade
and felt
         a power emanate from earth–
origins–
         massive waves like the magnetic
field flood over me,
                    invisible hands of
ancient belonging...
                    I am:

in this moment connected to all moments,
one body among many,
                    one face among
many,
     all over the changing world atoms
secretly singing
                music too high to hear,
each day born of quantum fire–
                              everyone

born from mysterious night,
                         from
swirling wings weaving together
time and space
                turning and rising from
an infinite coin in the dream waters
where I go to wish–
                    where many
masks dream each day lifted from
the faceless power
                stillness beneath all dreams...

    I once entered long ago
    a sacred shade serene,
    and then walked
    into the world
    and came to know
    all faces fall away
    into the night wind
    and night wind falls away
    into stillness–

And now I recognize my losses in the wind
that touches all faces, wind of absences
and erosions in the presence of many
in the presence of a faceless power behind
wind or rain and behind the masks of all faces...

                        And now–

what can I do but test the wind,
      its direction
and weather,
   though its future is always
indecipherable?–
     the carrier of history,
its journeys touch my face,
      a baptism
of distance–
    I am "a fugitive seeking asylum,"
hunting my home town:
      ancient soil,
dark loam
    I once gathered in my hand–

while the wars continue finding their range
past the bright flowers and birds– and I
return each night to the dream waters where
all the faces of time change their masks
and whoever I am seeks the infinite face
of the universe opening through my eyes,
whoever I am made of moonlight listens
for the first sharp cry across all centuries since–

though the earth deeply shifts and lightning
blazes like fierce syntax in the house of ghosts
and thunder talks out of the ages...

III

1.

A far crow cry out of another age,

the breeze swishing through aspens,

summer burning on the gravel roads,

dry crackling drone of grasshoppers
with the dust of the sun on their wings:

moments when all the gone and future days
collapse and time pauses, everything
balanced like a top on its motion–
                            and then
the clarity of childhood almost returns,
the world ablaze!–
                dancing light!–
but the lucid instant slips away,
its dark angel descends
like the flutter of a butterfly's shadow
glancing past the dark well of my pupil,
                                an age gone...

If these moments are nostalgia, they are
an autumn door that opens upon
the cellar of years the ghost of myself
yearns to descend, a stairs built from
the echoes of old stories—
                        calling
those shining days now dim,
                            ancient
flashes from another time,
                    a glimpse of myself
a child on the footbridge when afternoon light
crowned the dark river— and though
the river flowed and the light shifted
within the trees
                and the shadows lengthened
even as the fish swam toward twilight,
the world was neither old nor young
but certain,
          made of pure fire!

                2.

And still is.
        The sky is the same sky—

(though I've become stranger to myself,
a wandering scarecrow in a country
scared of itself,

                    the moon cold,
                                    indifferent...
I listen for the faint edge of a voice
in the season-eating wind,
                    a recognition...)

Still,
    in the stillness that resides beneath
cacophony and chaos,
                    in the undiminishing
quiet unending hour before dawn
pulls the colors out of night, the sky is
the same page it had always been,
open unwritten epic of each bright day...

    (each day an island between
    the past and the future, two faces
    of one nightmare my country fears,
    history's ghost haunting tomorrow)

Great sun rising over the world we've made,
whose walls broken or enduring define
the world we failed to erect,
                    ruins sinking
into the earth,
            ramparts and the prison walls
of history,
        the possessed land,
                    divided–

*(tell me: whose children mattered and whose
did not in the dream America made?)*–
                              fire-bound
sun rising over the sky-hung windows, towering
buildings, monolithic banks of San Francisco
whose streets the homeless wander,
                              all great cities
of the shining
              perishing republic!–
                      and villages
in other lands where the death birds came
roaring and left ashes, great sun rising over
those bombed homes, smashed windows without walls,
doors without houses, people without houses–
or the unbombed slums propped against
habit and the weather, one world divided
into power and need, the extremes of one people–
once-holy sun of our childhood daydreams,
hollering play, fire of origins!–
                         its light falls
and the shadows fall and *we are the day*,
bodies moving in the light in the stillness–
we are each the world,
                     all the open shouts
of children,
            each word spoken enters the wind–
we are the day falling toward the past where
everyone is equal under the same sky,
yesterday the same for everyone falling...

(And who doesn't want to look across the river
to the other side of the city— across the night
to the other side of the world where
others suffer— who doesn't believe
my suffering belongs also to the world?—
now I lay me down to sleep—
and almost hear other voices calling
out of millennial time—
       spirits...
          ancestors
whose echo I am...
        shuddering down
the long biological halls where   \
the hammer of the sea still thunders...)

One sunset I saw the river of light flow into sky–
I saw the red horizon gather all my days
and float them up into the dimming sky
toward the stars that speed and spend
the centuries, and in the oncoming darkness
I saw my life diminish across the wheat fields
like a canoe made of moonlight–
       the child I was...
gone...
  another age...
     gone...

      I saw
the sky that belongs to everyone together....
daydream

                who we are–
                          night dream–
who we were:
                    world we invent:
                                I saw
the light change–

                        3.

I came to exile,
              in my native land,
like a ghost haunting my own ground,
everything just out of touch,
a world locked within itself.

I wandered the streets of my town,
the day bright with flowers in the lawns,
a place at peace among the vegetables,
while at night the desperate dreams
of the citizens and their children
put on the faces of their rage
their wild rebellions and ranged
under the swimming constellations
like banshees nailed to the wind.

I roamed the city's edge, the country roads,
yearning to see the light shine
as the sun brightens and burns morning fog away:

the fields ignited in their own auras,
hawks blazing in their turns,
flicker tails a flurry of fire,
                              everything
electric in the communal light as if
the flash of a mirror could pass over the world
and return the clarity I once knew–
                                    but
some shadow had passed through my eyes
and each day was dimmed and dulled–
a nanosecond late as if the patina from light
had entered the air...

The world was washed and lost
in its own age–
                or I was lost in the wrong
country–
or my true self exiled in another land
flung far away–
                  an ancient child
I could no longer invoke
lurking behind my eyes,

who once walked the earth...

IV

1.

The uses of the day...
                      "I want to hold your hand"
(February 9, 1964)– while others were off to war.

Those times whose sound and cries and thunderous
deaths are long gone,
                  the smoke of that fury
was carried to the end of wind,
                      those days
whose uses were spoken from great guns:
"Give us this day our daily power," 500 pound bombs,
the tumbling tearing off-center seven-per-second
M-16 bullets:
          d-d-d-d-d-t d-d-d-d-d-t (sound of
snare drums of high school marching bands).

    And under the lunar drops of dew
    or gentle moon of rains, all those days
    went to sleep, the darkening rivers fell
    into the quicksilver sea, and the dead also
    went to sleep, in us– their eyes closed,

      their visions became equal to pebbles
      beneath the dark streams, blind
      to the days to come, the great turning fates,
      the drama of the immense stellar systems,
      the million million galaxies revolving,
      drifting, and our leaders' small dreams
      to rule one world– their myopic ambitions...

I can mention names, dates like someone who talks
in litanies like someone who talks inside the echo
of an empty cave–
                    with a diminishing voice
useless as a broken thread–
                        or I might talk
into a rusted can–
                or shout down a dry well–
but I might as easily talk about the channels
on Mars,
        or the erosions
                  the colored strata
of worn rock in the Bad Lands of North Dakota–

I might just as well try to capture a horse
made of mist in deep night as talk of days
gone and those that could have been,
worlds never born the same as the past
fallen away,
           a city blown apart the same
as a city never built in those days forgotten,
someone who died in the war forgotten

the same as photographs never taken
when the lunar light resides on waters
and human voices cease and sky once open
to questions is gone and no one asked
and no one answered why so many people
dove again and again into each dusk,
those soldiers gone who held child dreams
in their heads
                imaginary rooms
                                windows
open lakes
          ancient awe the sheen that slid
from a crow's wing
              light
                    another country
exploded flowers become teeth
                          exploded
houses become the past
          and the politicians
spoke automatic words and machine guns spoke:
d-d-d-d-d-t   d-d-d-d-d-t   d-d-d-d-d-t!

I might as well ask why the sun
did not go black as ask why the poor
needed to be bombed who needed
so much,
       or why no artist can paint death
in trompe l'oeil though Presidents freely give it–
it is easier
          to proclaim the holy ghost

in the empty grocery bag, the nose of the wind
skating across the parking lot than call back
those days decades ago that could have been
without war!
          The thieves came,
the sons of Caesar's sons came,
they stepped out of the fires of tomorrow
gazing back over their shoulders at what
they would do,
              havoc was born in their eyes–
they came from the ruined future and created
smoke,
        and morning arrived destroyed–
they lied and then the bombs fell
upon the instantly forgotten peoples,
they said something happened at the Gulf of Tonkin
and they stole lives and now the dead are nothing,
as journalist Oriana Fallaci said, who was there
and saw and said:

                "Give us this day
                our daily massacre,"
                and said,
                " deliver us from pity,
                from love, from trust
                in man, from the teaching
                your Son gave us. As
                it has been good for nothing,
                it is good for nothing.
                Nothing and so be it."

But stepping past her despair she then said:
"Look for what's right because right exists;
if it doesn't exist you have to make it exist."

Driven to despair from the war, she said
those words, Italian journalist who later
lost her own war with rage, but in her youth
she was braver than most Americans
at home in their "home of the brave,"
who retreat into a religion of patriotism,
who laud like Horace the empire because
they fear the world and want to conquer
fear–
      but she in her youth saw the suffering
and tried to understand as the enemy we killed
became younger
              and younger
as our bombs fell and acres of forest
erupted with napalm,
                    she tried to answer it:

"you have to make it exist."

And so do I–
          I of the private nostalgic train
crashing with all the ghosts of history
into oblivion gorge!
              So do we all!

Because otherwise the dolmens of Stonehenge
signify no human hour but only
abandoned time,
    they track the stars
from the circle of emptiness,
      and Einstein's
debates with space are nothing
but the measure of a black hole
whose only event is collapse–

     And yet:
yet yet yet yet yet
    d-d-d-d-d-t!–
what can be done against the sound of...

There is no way to save any of those ruined lives–
or my own.
    Those years remain a long time
beyond my touch and a flower of ash opens
no blossom but a gray world,
      perhaps the dusk–
a train become shadow has no future– and I
no longer know whose hand I would hold
from those days,
    my hand reaching back
falls apart like dust, my fingers
like old vines disappear–
      all becomes
smoke and autumn and even as I write
my hand is consumed in its own living flame!

That lawn outside our school in my youth
one spring day after lunch when I thought
about all our days to come, hoping
they would come well for us all, we who thought
days were important,
                    when the scent of blossoming lilacs
was heavy,
          sweet,
                 and the cotton of the cottonwoods
drifted in the breeze,
                     and the breeze was spring
and light and I saw strolling the girl I loved
from a distance–
                fantasy of what I thought
love was–
         that moment!–
                      bright and calm
an island in a dark decade when far away
a book of ruins was being written
in another country where our jets stormed,
that memory,
            those days now ride
the skin of lightning flashing through
                                      ghostly skies–

shadows that once moved across the earth
cannot return,
              water cannot return
to the salt of those tears...

2.

A litany of dates...
                useless to the uses of the day . . .

That past that was once my future, days
now folded into their dark, that time
when voices spoke and were silenced,
when Malcolm X was x'd out (February 21, 1965),
when I was fifteen and the wrath of Watts erupted
(August 11, '65), the sons and daughters of slaves
speaking out–
            and later other cities– and
the Summer of Love came and went in '67,
singing of those flowers the earth dreamed
and the young watered with their dreams
who thought they could declare days free as light,
when the poets marched on the Pentagon
(October 21, '67) in a moment of public language,
and Martin Luther King never went home
(April 4, '68), and the police in Chicago rioted
against freedom of speech (August 25, '68),
and astronauts landed on the moon (July 20, '69)
and the young landed at Woodstock (August 15, '69),
still singing as if they could declare themselves
free as light,
            and I was older than I was
and have been ever since, as we all were

who wanted to hold a hand not a gun– and
the moon
        scales a cold vigil over the cities
and that time is gone and best left buried
with the dead who are nothing in time now–

except:

      they once lived, they came and died,
they came and the blue spaces of the future
where they thought they would build their days
entered their young eyes– all those soldiers
sent to die and the Vietnamese soldiers they killed–
their days voyaged on hope– they came and lost
as we fear losing and they died and beyond
their touch our future opened as they fell away,
as the ground became solid where we stepped
beyond their lives– they fell through the world
and our days floated on their absence–
                                and time
flowed from their shadows like oceans into our nights . .

                3.

And I would gather all the moths of the world
if I could– under the nimbus of the moon
and on their autumn-colored wings
sprinkled with the dust of the earth,
                              call home

the whisper of those lives,
                          each last breath,
to a still lake whose shores begin to stir
with the gentle hum of those wings–
                          and
in that deep drone out of the eons a rumor
of another world this one
                          might become–
and then:
            holding in my hand a river-worn rock
the size of my palm,
                    cool skin of the past
made smooth and anciently new by baptism
in that long wash,
                    I would dream the world flung
into a new time across the dark waters, the ages
of its terror,
            the abiding silence,
                        like a singing stone.

V

1.

Could a stone sing in a poem
could a poem bring me home
could lunar moth-light last
or lost horizons be recast?

Gravity has its way,
    O deeply down!–
        through the strata
of the centuries,
   cities buried beneath cities–
and distance tears all long nostalgias apart!

At long last I stepped beyond the endless, those wide open
free vistas of childhood, living rooms made of fields,
sun-capped knolls of eternal pause,
       and left behind
those times and time slid on and away,
slipping on an avalanche of horizontal shadows
into all the days before!–
      and yesterday is shuffled

like a card played out, whether good or bad luck,
as wind reshuffles the surface of water and water
calms and captures like a woman's eyes
the light skimming across ancient mysteries.

But–
    if I hunt the lost light of my days joined to those
of all my ancestors whose time entered this land,
if I could levitate the dead to dance on the thin
star-flung waves of glacier-carved lakes of Minnesota
and all the waters of the world so wide and wild,
or if the slender awns of wheat in the fields could shudder,
or a stone flung across the waters could secretly sing,
or moth-wings that fly all the dark avenues of night
hum like one note with the secrets of the past,
could my senses make sense of the disappeared worlds
that once ranged and raged?–
                      now disguised behind
this world that keeps rising to wave farewell to itself–
all those days vaguely slipping into history
(that great maw)
            beyond the western edge where
all empires,
      their light, dark and dust,
                  end?

2.

At last the war ended–
                in Vietnam–
the war transformed into the smoky, the mystical
days of memory where terror becomes
the dance of diaphanous shadows fading
away,
        the net of the past breaking apart...

But it also moved like a stealthy cloud, a sullen
nest of secret thunder gathering in other skies–
moved to Nicaragua which threatened Texas,
drug-dealer Reagan said– remember the sacred
mission, guard the Alamo and the bones of Bowie!–
and then moved to Grenada which threatened
to beat up American students,
                        that poor beat up country–
and then to Panama,
                and then the war for oil
in Iraq,
     movie produced by Bush and Son Incorporated,
while the war against the Palestinians continued
and monstrous Sharon, Butcher of Beirut Sabra Shatila,
remanufactured the Warsaw ghetto with U.S. gun ships,
Israel worth six aircraft carriers, Senator Helms said.
The war went wherever the colonies of the poor
rebelled against the empire.

                  The war that ended
without ending continued without cease
everywhere against the poor,
                  the daily war
more dependable than bread continued–
and the poets in the alcazar of the academy...
they had their say...
                  did their duty and protested
according to the fashion of the day–
                  and then
decided history was done.

                  History was
a hollow fallen owl left over from winter
tumbling through its own blind snowy time,
useless wings,
                  history was without a flag
as it has always been,
                  history was
the jagged shards of a jar in another country
nameless,
                  history was
the weapon that ate itself in its own rust,
slow cold fire of cast away steel–
                  history was
someplace the poets of the empire forgot
to remember,
                  history was six million year old
Toumai skull on the Djurab desert,

ancient hope of life too far away to matter–
even as the poor in their own country were
too far away and beyond all necessary words...

Who were the poor?–
                        broken not by bullets
but simply forgotten–
                        the homeless Viet Nam
veterans who wandered the past, ghosts
daily resurrected in their own bodies
(passing through a dusk mirror, their frayed
army coats the color of autumn)–
                                history became
a stubbled field full of swirling remnants
of another season, became the sun's chaff
meaningless–

        And the poor remained among us–
without meaning. The poor, who proclaimed
nothing,
        remained among themselves,
came and went among their own voices
forgotten,
        who could not forget themselves...

        Who would want to know
        what it means to be unknown,
        a shadow captured within
        the moon's penumbra– "who?"
        the ghost of last year's owl

      asks in the hollow of the wind,
      would want to know a nation
      made of days made of dead
      ends, days of empty pockets,
      worn shoes, worn-out words,
      silence– who would want to know
      the castaways, the throwaway
      children of the empire,
      the internal outcasts of
      the homeland insecurity,
      who would want to walk into
      the dark at the edge of the tilth
      where bucolics are absurd,
      edge of the American Dream,
      exile of one's own land,
      who would want to know
      a history made from shadows?

Those people of the ungiving past of the hungry
future,
      who would want to enter that nation,
abandoned people abandoned to anger–
cities of secret fires blossoming their dreams
expired flowers tearing themselves
apart,
      explosions!–
            but not the engulfing
form-hating fires of war that invent
white-hot doors and shatter air
with too sudden light–

                  these explosions
unwind in slow ferocities...
                angers
that reside and abide *in* the light,
the colors of the day,
        do not cease–
               who
would want to know what the poor
know,
    enduring but angry,
           but longing
as the wind is long,
        but angry,
              open
as the sky is wide–
        but angry–
            vast
as the stars are distant–
        but poor?

Ancient hope of life– Toumai skull–
history...
        eyes hollow with all the time
of the past, all the time of the future,
the lunar night asleep on the great desert–
origins...

"War is energy Enslaved," says Blake

and energy enslaved remains at war...

3.

Others came before–
I felt their movements
arranging the dark
in the deep recesses of night...

They carved petroglyphs,
anchored their times in rock,
but wind and water unspell
all names– time's allies
erode the day from
beneath its wish and want.

Could a stone sing
in a poem, could song
rise through all
our nights from
the ancient waters,
awaken far ages–

could ageless eyes of
Toumai skull six million
years ancient look through
my eyes– anciently nascent
light of the moon's wash–
could lost horizons be
recast, lunar moth-light
last, or our lasting

needful losses begin
a world no one owns,
ancient hope of life,
ancient hope of... light?

Could a world answer
those silent signs carved
in rock across millennia–
a world hear itself at last
in wind everywhere
the same– speak from
summers winters that once
needed to be, from time's
long call,
            call itself home?

VI

1.

In the always drifting out lands vanishing
nightly from under my feet, I tried to homestead
eternal summer,
    feast of the bright day
for foolish children themselves food
of the passing seasons–
      lake-sheen and
flower-shimmer,
    those fields of corn sun-stung
storing the light like nuggets of noon
perpetual in their banks of green envelopes
and my home address in the universe
1003 Pine Street Marshall Minnesota
where I roamed and worried but was also home.

Youth so hard to lose because it is all we know.
That country held me...

    And still does:
      Camden,

Lake Marshall,
               the unnamed ponds and gravel
pits where the heavy shadows of carp loitered
on the shallow bottom,
                   the waters gleaming
under open sky,
            those fields ablaze!–
                       earth become
soul,
    that prairie,
          all the lay and hay of the land
remains but nothing remains,
                  gone like
a continent sunk beneath this one, fallen
into the mythical geography of an ancient sun...

And that country's name is not America,
not pronounced by *patres conscripti* dividing
their abstract atlas into real estate, but
perhaps spoken in some forgotten time zone,
the deep center of beginnings, the nonsense talk
and free grammars of small children, musical
gibberish like the babble and murmur of rivers...

I remember when I was a teenager, perhaps
fifteen, seeking refuge in woods on a hillside
overlooking a creek. Studying nothing,
trying to know nothing,
                  the wide calm...

I wanted to locate a place where time condensed,
a moment like a glint of light from quartz
opening into the wide world beyond
the secret cave of myself and the pain
the small and large murders of my unquiet
careless kind–
            unkind carriers of a dark
and dangerous dread–
                  of each other–
                          being hunted–
afraid of the hungry eyes of the poor.

I wanted the transparent air to come
alive,
      awake and these people free
                   open
                        clear:
the way I saw the afternoon light flash upon water!

Then I saw a young buck sturdy with his spring
antlers,
      unsure he should cross the brook,
sniffing for scent and what fate ruled
on the other side,
           unsure as we all are
in the terrible dream of the killing world!

A slight breeze stirred the new leaves
in the tall poplars and elms.

                    For a long time
he listened,
          all his senses alert like crystal fire!
He *was* his senses–
          but what else too?

What at the center calls to be saved?

I snapped a twig,
          he bolted!–
                  clambered up
the opposite hill!–
          gone over the crest as if
absorbed in air! That was forty years ago
and he is long dead. And all those from the war.

Why do we keep those deer in those lands
where light leapt out of our lives?

                2.

I went back to my home town after
twenty years.
          Who can return
to their native ground without facing
jealous suitors?– but unlike Odysseus,
all avatars of oneself–
                survivors

of earlier struggles,
            each battle fought
for dear life also a loss—
            even victory
a blow because someone had to lose,
someone was hurt—
            somewhere
through all the nights of the earth
dark masks crashed to the heavy beat
of remote drums—
            or perhaps only
the hollow waves of the ocean— or
rhythm of thunder, ancestral memory—
perhaps while crossing the street a flash
of a lone child beneath the moon who
wonders why survival is important.

            And yet: the body
doesn't wonder, the body with all its darkness
continued to step into the light, into the street
however badly beaten the spirit,
            and rose
with its name like a necessary shield to face
the next conflict,
            whether sport or dispute,
basketball or battle, everyone hunting
some kind of triumph, a moment free to itself
like a bright wing suspended and no one
inscribed on the back of a plaque the old rule:
"victory and defeat gnaw at each other

in the marriage of a carking riddle"–
because someone had to lose even as
the cup that falls to the ground shatters
and the earth revolves through its shadow
erasing the great actions of each day.

I rebelled. I was weary of the catechism:
win! win! win! What was the purpose?
Who wins and who loses, who's in
and who's out? I was depressed,
I wanted to reverse the rules and lose.
Would I receive a garland of dried weeds?
Would my name diminish in value?
Who were the losers in the Hall of Oblivion
where I knew in time there was redemption
for all winners? At the track meet I ran
and ran the relay but I knew I would quit.
I was an automaton putting foot in front
of foot until half way to the finish
I allowed the long gloom of my solitudes
like blue lead to enter my muscles.
Without spirit the body is cumbersome
weight and the distance to the ground grew.
I stretched forward on the heavy stilts
of my legs but at last gave up fighting
myself and trudged from the field,
a volunteer in the league of losers,
but freed from the need to win– empty
in the disgrace of my satirical disdain
for glory. The coach and team were furious!

I did not care. I wore the mask of night.

I was like the elephants of grief who revisit
the bones of their deceased, and toss them
and bellow and cry and wonder
what has become of their powerful companions,
what are these bones that belong to the moon?

And still survival fashioned a face against
the abrading wind even as the wind
erodes the enduring rock wall, even as
the rock wall is unable to vanish,
the one at Camden or at Pipestone.
The rock wall cannot say:
> "I'd rather not be here.
>   I'd rather not cast
>   a deep shadow."

Going back is a meeting with yourself
and unlike Odysseus, you always lose.

> The old school house is gone,
> its stairs are passages to rooms
> whose floors are air. The slab
> for high jumping remains
> but the field is no longer
> used and those great leaps
> are the prowess of the young
> who think the old are foreigners
> from the land of discarded clocks.

    The driveway to the house
    leads to another day
    when we played basketball
    in October 1962
    and wondered if the world
    would blow up. The world
    didn't blow up but departed
    by its usual method.

Power and loss...
                     However we look
at each day,
            and day slipping west,
or listen to the music of the day,
bird chatter or rhythm of words,
or give hand to another hand
though neither holds the day,
or whether we believe nation will last
as if flags are never eaten by wind,
the power the glorious day fades,
leaks through the gauze of each sunset
like a mirage finding the wound of its escape,
and someone behind our eyes
both old and young, someone
haunted by age and youth equally,
faces the abyss of all time and wonders
why survival means power and power
is important, why rust gathers
in the hinge of the door or the door
falls upon the earth, and the night

and the door become the same...

But wonders anyway because wonder
thinks it knows something else,
the dream light of the wishing well,
meditation from which the day rose...

I didn't return only to recall the town,
its river, familiar streets, the nagging
memories, but learn again a transparency
I once knew.

      And though I felt again
the crystal black knives dive through
the city night I once wandered restless
while the lamps burned in their glass cages
as if beneath a heavy sea–

                in those years
when I wondered at my difficulty talking,
or why no one said the urgent things...

and though the crickets in evening
now sang exile,
         and the alfalfa fields
were now bean,
         and the gravel road
now tar,
     and the corn fields had given way
to houses,

        and the poplars were gone
from my back yard,
           this soil,
                this history,
the prairie,
       this town revealed itself
like gates of a mirror parting,
              opening
across time and a strange thing happened:
though I was an exile in my home land,
                I was
also home:
      I stepped into a place I had forgotten.

I felt invisible,
      free,
        a dancer
in the center of energies,
         I was
light absorbed in light,
          my aura reached
all emanating auras,
          my shadow knew
the earth and felt the long touch of shadows...

In the day complete and whole
I found again the place of recognitions–

or walked through a spinning stillness where
I could disappear as a character from

The Book of Ruins and enter the instant
that knew all seasons– and I walked
my native land like a place I've always known
where the converging of the curving horizons
suspended the floating dream of the town
in the same endless moment always one.

I visited the graveyard where we once ran
and played under those swaying branches
that cast shadows among the polished
monuments carved with those hollow years
we traced with our fingers as if we could touch
that dead history we thought so far away.

The dry ancient drone of the cicadas
drilled through the summer afternoon
as though all those years of absence
were five minutes ago– and I had never left.
They buzzed me back into blazing light,
home in the center of my knowing.

But this was one day in twenty years.

When I departed in the early fog
driving away from the land where
the soul of my childhood is stored,
mourning doves flew out of the mist
like three white bolts from nowhere,
almost smashing into my windshield
as if trying to kill themselves,

first one,
        then another,
                and again!–
as if warning me, somehow,
of the dangers of returning.

Or: they might have been only
three mourning doves lost
like myself in the fog of time.

3.

No one can go back– all the myths say so.

And also teenagers who think
yesterday's dream will be tomorrow's light,
and speak as if they knew,
gathered at dusk in the parking lots,
or in the alleys or on country roads,
in their youth still convinced somehow
the next day knows them. They need
their belief. But for all their bravado
they are scared.
        The roads are all open
into the future,
        as far as the next step
and then–
        the great unknown night...

For my generation the next step was war.

It's hard to know: is the atomic bomb
the same as a peony in God's eye,
those explosions of color in the dawn?

We learned fire and then deep in the earth
we disturbed the sleeping power of the sun's
nuclear hive,
            but even before the efficient
furnaces of Hiroshima and Nagasaki
not even Shadrach, Meshach, Abednego
could survive,
            the napalming of Royan, France
by 1200 B 17s– a city of no threat–
a military experiment,
                    the future of power...

We've learned the secrets of frost
building its roads on windows–
but who are the ghosts of ourselves?

Even if we've always known what the world
wanted us to become, we've lacked
the spare change to pay for it:
                  the infinite
coin of shifting light
            struck by moon glow
in the wishing well
            of ancient waters

where all potential of the universe roils,
and yin and yang
                   circle like two unborn
phantoms,
        we forgot to imagine...

How can anyone mention: "Here,
take this strange coin I saw in a dream,
it is free, this imaginary token in my hand,
this day between us–
               and the rest of the world?"

It could be anything, a smooth stone,
translucent agate we loved as kids, or
nothing but a pool of dream-captured light–

Who could buy bread with such a coin?

History, with its wars over other coins,
had no time for such open accounts...

And now our Commander-in-Chief the Deserter
dispenses fire again and those perennial
young die again, who have no money.

And hope, whose flag would be blue
if it had one,
         goes on wishing for that country
where other worlds seemed possible–
                     nostalgia,

Narcissus of Time,
                    sets up camp just beyond
the horizon in the valley of "remember me,
remember us– our generation and times..."
the most futile cause on earth...

The legacy of my days here–
                    and also
of my tribe–
          is no peaceful dream.
                              Nature
did not say as some merry poets suggest:
"go to sleep, dream of harmony, be content,"
 but it said:
          "*I am made of teeth antlers and claws,
*softness protected in armor, the weather is absolute,
the quaking earth and sky without compassion*"–
and then we made knives and cruise missiles
and war was rearranging metal and debris–
and smoke,
          the ghost of ruins,
                              climbed the wind.

Was the only other choice to lie down
beneath a wave of grass and let
all the gold of autumn eat our hearts?

They were always the barbarians who
conspired in the shadows that gathered
on the other side of each conquered day,

they moved in the darkness of our fear,
heathens, savages: who were they?–
demons cloaked in the twilight,
brothers and sisters we refused to know...

We called it "our way of life..."
though life had its own way.

And so we go on spending money
as if time and spirit can be frozen
in metal coins, fate ruled by inheritance,
and the empire will last forever...

VII

1.

Out of all the ages of ourselves,
wanderings and wars, we arrive at this age
when we might extinguish the woven fire
passed down the centuries, DNA strands
stranded in time– the passing of
the encrypted kinetics that carry life...

Power seems to decide all matters– it is
the way the universe was made:
the surge of the first instant smashes
the void, ameba eats ameba, the deer fly
torments the deer but is innocent,
the avalanche crashes its mass of snowflakes
that drifted one by one calmly from
the passive sky– nothing stands in the way.

And for us: the empire. How long
since the camps moved from the rivers
and sentinels stood at the gates of the city?
If thunder answers deep ocean silence,
it also announces the secret caverns of the rose

but what did we hear except
long drums echoing down the emptiness?

And in the center of that cacophony
and passion for power, is there a dreaming
seed a folded world clenching the silence
against all contradicting tongues, another future
where the desperate poor change their face?

Power and chance seem to decide–
not justice, not kindness, need, care,
compassion... neither the single-purposed virus
that duplicates itself by cellular coup d'etat
nor the atomic bomb whose single word
speaks its own demise, cares about potential saints.

These are the darkest ages, I've decided,
where all crises intersect like critical mass,
without knowing what ages will follow,
if any– but the Great Systems: winds,
rains, rivers, even the tribe of deer flies–
are greater than any powers we invent.

Can power pause in a universe whose law
is power? We might cease killing but that idea
requires eyes clear with the light of the world
and my compatriots would rather wave flags.

Still– there is another law. The universe
is also a vast mirror, unbreakable–

like water, like air– and what we throw
returns– and perhaps this law is justice
though our atom-splitters cannot find it.

The air and water give back our poisons,
the rich take the money and build prisons
but enslave themselves behind their fences,
the missile punches into the center of zero
and bursts and kills and flames spread
their bright wings over buildings and fly
from existence– and yet the heart of fire
plants a small seed, particle of darkness,
condensed fear that falls back through time
and pulls all history into itself and opens
visions of starless nightmare where monsters
throw rocks at each other's eyes and cannot talk.

> The warrior comes to Hakuin, Zen master.
> "Is there a heaven, a hell?" he asks.
> Hakuin provokes him. "You are unshaven.
> I see you have a sword– it is probably rusty!"
> The warrior, offended, draws his sword.
> "Here!" Hakuin says. "Open the gates of hell."
> The warrior resheathes his sword.
> "Here!" Hakuin says. "Open the gates of heaven."

Can nations sheathe their swords?

Today I read in *The Wallstreet Journal*
the unelected twice installed President

(himself AWOL from the Viet Nam War)
is no caesar– the republic needs to be told
as he gathers the nation's armies...

A strange universe the rational scientists
agree.
      Great beasts in space, their energies
so immense ten billion years of our sun's power
flashes in one second:
              supernovae and also
the dark vanishing points where
collapsed stars have fallen through time:
black holes–
      and here:
           on this ground:
missiles bombs napalm like all the wrath
and wraiths of the past imprisoned in fire–
violent transposition of cities,
              energy,
energy,
      an empire of colonial tyrants
and corporations,
      labor,
          gravity and grief,
wealth and death
      this age of America is
a tiny flicker,
      passing firefly,
          a spark
flung against the deep void of the tall galaxies–

though it be powerful like all previous
empires built upon the lives of the poor,
(those children on porches of rented wrecks
of homes,
        or street urchins killed by police
in Argentina Columbia,
                nuisances without jobs),
the empire of the oligarchy that would rule
the world is only a flurry
              of dust
under
      the indifferent swirl of stars.

              2.

Great beasts in space– and our own
bêtes noires here,
        secretive fears...

Can the national symbols:
              flags,
                  eagles,
medallions,
      anthems,
             one nation under
a patriotic God,
        save us from the fear
of falling off the edge of the world?

When did you first learn your life
was unnecessary,
    your voice did not matter
to the silence,
    the rivers would flow,
leaves fall without you,
    even meteors
once lucky stars–
    and some atavistic shape
huge as a spruce stepped from deep forests,
a nightmare walking on a carpet of dead
butterflies,
    crystal eyes shining with infinity–
Kali,
  Shiva,
    satirical Satan the other face of God,
a presence fatal to the illusion of the world?

We are driven by hunger. As soon
as we enter the world we begin eating it–
the law is: dine or die.   And world
surrounds us,
    public and unpredictable!

Perhaps wind is a chrysalis of unimagined
creatures calling...
    but in time time locates
the vanishing point of diamond and distance...

I suppose I could say easily enough

most are devoted to things as if things
could save, loving speed as though speed
were escape, jet skis churning emptiness,
snowmobiles whining down the frozen
rivers like long snakes trying to shed
the skin of time, even as the waters
beneath continue cold and silent.

Time!
       All unfolds in the drama of time!
The history of life: hunger, survival,
the first cell the first urge in the shape of zero,
life's mandate: to avoid becoming nothing,
and later: the organized hunger of nations...

Those tanks in the city parks are not glory
but were made to kill. Several million years
from Oldowan tools to megaton bombs:
all that time honing the calculations of power!

Once we fought fascism but that was
some years ago. Now young charming girls
in fatigues but without weariness smile
bright for photographs over tortured prisoners.
There are those who resolve the nation
is blessed by God but no children are born
with the word "America" on their lips.

They know another country without flag
or name but like ourselves learn to forget.

At the end of the echo of our call
down the ages,
              lunar light strikes the water
of the wishing well but we awaken and forget.

I saw the patriotic sign: *"Pride Power Peace"*
and wondered if all three words could be loaded
into the cannons, how peace rises from ruins?

What is the song of pride and power?

      We don't need forests, let's cut them down.
      We don't need birds, let's divide the sky.
      We don't need the poor, let them starve.
      We don't need mice, sew them together
      for coats, we don't need wind, it brings
      bad news, but how to stop it? We don't need
      blood bone soul or song of our brother
      but what is that dark bird in the mirror
      flying away through the eye's pupil?

Our true country will come as surprise,
like all necessities...
                  from loss...
                            from
those great distances–
              voices fading away...
a nation,
      a myth,
            a memory that had power

yesterday as if the West were not a crucible
but a promised land even as the buffalo fell,
those ancient beings,
                              in those hooves silence...

Money is not the coin of that realm.

    The quarter lifted from wet soil
    leaves behind its imprint equal to
    all the centuries reduced to zero.
    It was captured all winter in ice
    useless to the economy. The sky
    pours into the shape of its absence.
    It doesn't matter, once gone,
    what was there: a quarter or
    the rarest element on earth. It is all
    the same, it is nothing, a sliver of air
    so thin it could be a last breath or
    the hollowness in bas relief of everything
    the country has failed to become,
    the openness of the world...

By night the moon mints its own coin.

Photographs,
              pieces of wood,
                              mementos,
letters of the dead,
              letters to ourselves,
nothing we save saves–

                    but a dark current
flows beneath all that ancient ink,
beneath all those preserved images,
and the people we remember turn back
in early dawn, unwilling to remain caught,
and in time a fatal touch will pass
through the illusion of this world,
through ourselves,
                and then?–

Then the moon rises through our own
distance,
            through our long absence
of people who left,
                and rivers flow
with the absence of all our ancestors
who roamed the earth,
                    a moment round
in luminous silence rises huge over
the dark roiling oceans–
                and then
there is no longer need for power,
nothing to grab,
            and wind talks to wind–

Then we come to mystery...

where time reveals its reverse face
and the nations we built are memory of
the world we forgot to imagine...

And the empire that traded on the loss
of others has already collapsed,
      fallen
from power in the round moment that is,
though not yet by our measure of time...

The empire tried to assault time and found
only time,
   trained its cannons its cruise missiles
on the rose but the blossom merely died
and nothing could be stolen from it–
the glowing illusion its beauty became brittle
and for those who wanted to possess it,
bitter–

The empire built on nothing is built on
all past empires become nothing:

the staircase we climb and have been
climbing all this long history
is shadow falling away beneath us,

and broken stone step by broken
skyscraper
    the serene moon ascends.

3.

The moon lifts over my home town,
lifts then and lifts now, once when
I was there and now when I am not.

The moon lifts over that place
long before my home town
sank foundations into that prairie
where the river meandered without
the shadows of bridges upon those waters,

the moon lifts and shines upon that land
before it was my home and also lifts
in other nights I shall never see,

that same light soft ancient strikes
the waters, the moon rises over
all our sleep through ages
where ancestors were and we are,
it lifts over oceans and estuaries
and the luminous silence rises
to reside over all nations.

At last at end of day century millennium
we are left with moonlight and earth.
We are left with a glass of water,
moonlight, and ourselves, the absence of
some we knew and some we denied,

we are left with our fate when we look
into our past, we are left with moonlight,
our hands, our need to touch, and earth.

Dog that howls at the moon,
poetry that would if it could speak
the syllable of the moon, drop of dew
mixed with darkness, the communal O
that travels like hollowness in the wind,
that we almost speak in love in silence
struck by each other, sounding the depths
of soundless places when the silence
is whole when the moon calls us from
our bodies from within ourselves
through our bodies to unite with ourselves
under the moon– and all our memories
and possessions dissolve and walls
and horizons fall away and we
fall through ourselves and our lost lands
as the moon rises through emptiness
in its pure circular hour through
all our lives that will be forgotten
by those who will also be forgotten
in time as time forgets us all, and forgets
great nations– through our absence
the moon through the center of ourselves
country without name
                              rises and shines...

VIII

1.

Rachel Corrie

I begin from my home town, that soil
where once my hands planted seed,
but my words locate in another land,
Rafah, Gaza,
        where
someone born three decades later
died.

     And now I know the dark
in the deepest ocean floor is the same
as the dark on the far side of the moon.

Now I know exile is not a place lost, exile
is not measured in years or distance,
but a word unspoken, a voice silenced.

Who stood against the demolition of homes
in an occupied city, who was Rachel Corrie,
who put herself between guns and victims,

"the difficulties the Israeli Army would face
if they shot an unarmed U.S. citizen,"
who stood against the exile of people
in their own land in a land not hers,
Rachel Corrie, 23, from Olympia, Washington,
murdered in the afternoon in Rafah, Gaza?

*In this world of works
only in body lives the word,
only in blood and bone
the spirit of the word works.*

A forty nine ton bulldozer, a blade eight feet tall,
against the body of a young woman– who gave
the word to bulldoze Rachel Corrie under earth?

*In this world of words
without meaning without works
what words invoke the spirit,
what works deny the world?*

Writing to her mother she said:
"I don't know if many of the children here
have ever existed without tank-shell holes
in their walls and the towers of an occupying
army surveying them constantly from
the near horizons... An eight-year-old
was shot and killed by an Israeli tank
two days before I got here, many
of the children murmur his name– Ali–

tanks and bulldozers destroyed
25 greenhouses– livelihoods for 300 people...
I see orchards and greenhouses and fruit trees
destroyed... welfare completely strangled...
a shrinking place...   This is not at all
what I asked for when I came into this world.
This is not at all what the people here
asked for when they came into this world.
This is not what I meant when I looked
at Capital Lake and said:
'This is the wide world and I'm coming into it.'"

> *Who gave the word,*
> *whose word gave spirit*
> *to the work to destroy*
> *Rachel Corrie, who spoke*
> *the word that moved*
> *forty nine tons toward murder,*
> *whose wish would be*
> *the word that would take*
> *from the wide world*
> *the spirit of Rachel Corrie?*

She escorted children to school in Rafah
so Sharon's army would not shoot them,
the word she said: "This has to stop."

The word Blake said: *"War is energy Enslaved."*

In Rafah three of six wells bulldozed, water,

water– in the light of the Army snipers,
her shadow fell among those of workers
trying to repair the wells of Rafah–

                                          because
the wells of Rafah could not cast up
song a mystical cyclone deep voices of the past
to turn away the bulldozers, she was there,
Rachel Corrie from Olympia with its vast
Capital Lake–
                water:

    on the wide earth what people
    live without water, where are
    people anywhere on earth who live
    on wind, the memory of water?

"Not at all what people asked for when they came
into this world," when we come into this world,
each of us a wish born from its infinite well–
we ask for the world– she offered the world
itself, herself its coin and word.

And then came the lies about her death,
"a regrettable accident," though all witnesses
say no. What is a lie but murder of word?

Her life, like everyone's a moment sustained,
she lost its balance on that mound of dirt,
eye to eye with driver whose eyes became

blind machine that refused to pause
and rolled up the earth as though breath
were sand and steel the law of God:
whose word closed earth over Rachel Corrie's sky?

Between workers and tanks: Rachel Corrie.
Between child and sniper: Rachel Corrie.
Between a doctor's house and bulldozer...

Rachel Corrie died in a land not hers– though
home to horizons where no land is foreign.

Now when I look into the dark of each day past
where we all must gather alone and together,
I think she is moonlight that comes to all, *Shahid*
of us all, who touched the world like moon
finds its soul on water, from tarn to estuary
and all ocean-wide, moonlight where world
dreams a world renewed, and no country's exile.

2.

> Imagination is surrounded by
> the daughters of Inspiration,
> who in the aggregate are call'd
> Jerusalem.
> —William Blake

In the twilight the sand hill crane,

the great blue heron, hunt in the marshes,
beavers patrol the rivers, pipers flit
over calm waters lacquered with sky,
deer browse the salads of the earth
like shy connoisseurs born from dusk,
the night-masked raccoon or armored
porcupine, their nations without
prophets, quislings or saviors, follow
the habits of their tribe's ancestry–
great waves of instinct move through
the wild populations of the earth.

I don't know the depths of their studies,
their conversations with earth and its ages...

But for my kind, who stepped into sunlight
and uttered words like "footprint," "continent,"
"empire"– even recklessly "moon"– what
can the passing of time mean, millennia
condensing like some unworldly element
floating in its own realm on the edge
of tomorrow, that uncorrupted country?

How long since we pulled metals
from the earth and honed them into
potentials of velocity?
                              And now there are
citizens impatient to be saved from
a universe that saves nothing, praying
as if centuries had decided it is time

the greatest nation of the moment
mass its tanks to invade the sunset.

When the great speeches were made
how many ruined houses were forgotten?
The gypsum board of walls turned to chalk
and joined solidarity with ancient cities,
and windows,
          carrying streams of fire,
flew horizontally between the thin edge
of day and night where no one can distinguish
the first dawn from the last dusk.

And though we forget how all roads
that led to this moment were built
by disturbing the ancient clays,
and neglect to remember our tradition has been
clowns of tragedy dancing upon the bones
of those we've killed,
          we cannot forget
tomorrow has no face and forgives nothing,
and cares nothing for prophets who are dust,
already propping up flashes of sunlight
like blind mirrors upon the noon lakes.

And if I look to the gates of the future
I see fire flung out of the first dawn
into night the destroyer of the past!–
on the western horizon where all energy collects
like ferocious wasps devouring themselves,

in a feast of delirium the altitudes of sky
incinerated–
         and cities burning in the long light
our blind windows burning and sacred symbols
flags of cliché and plastic dashboard christs,
all slide west falling into dusk where the cross
of the past and future lingers in flame
at the intersection of war and dream–
and all holy ghosts in robes of fire!–
                        Jerusalem
burns down
         and its latest conqueror
Saturno Sharon that gluttonous monstrosity
consumed by passions to possess the earth,
devourer of children
              whose hungry dead eyes
become ash the grave of the world where
swirling light sinks into pits of darkness,
and the long reign of despots falls through time
into black holes that oversee ruin,
                 and a funereal
navy blazing and all the long dead of history
voyage out to the cold heaven of the stars...

Uruk, Babylon, Tyre, Athens, Carthage, Paris,
London, Washington D.C., all great cities in flame,
blazing as the day burns down!–
                   the Eternal
City of Light burning and all ephemeral capitals,
their power and legacies,

                        glory of flags and emblems
obliterated!–
            their laws unwritten by spontaneous
flaming pens,
            all fenced paradises guarded by
fiery angels,
            the skies of America the Empire of Despair
torn down in the failing light–
                        and the British Empire,
and the Holy Roman Empire
                        and the one before,
and I see Alexander the Great Lost One
trying to conquer sand or Shi-Hwang-ti
first universal emperor whose Great Wall
walled out the universe, all kings and khans,
tzars, caesars, kaisers, imperial potentates,
shahs, rajahs, gaekwars, moguls, thakurs,
fakers, presidents supreme and ministers prime,
truncated Ozymandias, Napoleon the Deserter,
mad ranting Hitler, Bush the Petty Conqueror,
the husk of Sharon–
            burning as Jerusalem burns–
"Jerusalem is become a ruin"– "Shiloh is in ruins"–
and the Buddhist monks motionless collapse
in flame– the forests of Viet Nam explode again,
the works of the day burn down, the bloody
passions of the power mongers roil and glow
whose language speaks in tongues of fiery corrosion
burn dance and burn in their own histories...

* * * * *

Even as I see Jerusalem rise beyond itself–
without name or nation give itself away–
dying flames of molten glass slipping into air,
the window of the sunset dissipating into dusk,
the last light building shelves in the lofts of clouds
where the waters already know the dark–
and all cities and villages become
                              one world,
Jerusalem, Rafah, Marshall, Laporte, Canby–
and rivers wandering the dark without countries
and the secret waters of Walden and Camden...

Tomorrow if it comes will not forget the fires
we failed to build on the shores of its birth–
glowing hours we saw in the mirror of our past,
on the circular rim of the world, citadels
of light thrown back into our imagination,
sheer cities lifted on wings of cool flame,
in the Capitol of Conflagrations, *energies freed*...

When the great speeches were made
what did power signify when the moon rose
to put the day to sleep and all the weapons
dreamed in their steel severity of metal fatigue?

                              3.

And as moon rides the ocean
where shadows sleep inside waves

that rise and fall inside the sleeping world
and the masks of time rise and fall,
faces of ourselves falling inside
the shadows of waves and the faces
of the world see each other
in the transparency of water,
faces of water falling into faces of water
as the lunar shadows fall into each other
where the waters of yesterday and those
of tomorrow rise and fall the same
in their sleeping worlds— and rivers
corridors of time lose themselves
in the estuaries and the Sea of Tranquility
shines upon the ocean of shadows,
the ocean of faces falling in the past
or in the future inside the falling waves
of the sleeping world— and as the dark
shelves of the continents rise and we
rise to our shores in the light
of our waking, who can say where
we have been without our knowing?

And in this sudden moment, this power
of our lives when we are flames walking,
passions speaking, fear hiding in its masks,
and there is only a brief time to say
a valuable word— *what at the center calls?*—
what calls from the center of each
vibrating wave of energy: inside
the dark of stone or within the wind

that resides in trees— or the voices
of children declaring the world, or
the meditation of a gardener who imagines
flowers are birds poised for flight,
or lovers who consume each other
by those private but public soaring fires,
how does the world call to itself,
cities born out of all the cities of the past,
and yesterday's shadows become ours,
and the sky's thin blue expanse sliding west
where antediluvian beasts drag the day down?

And as the most ancient world the moon rises
over the earth and locates in the rivers of dream
apparitions like dissolved clouds of the day,
who can bulldoze lunar light into a hill
and climb all the centuries and proclaim:
"I own the past and all that shall come,
I own the oceans of origins and the rain.
Before the wells of the world I will lean together
two shin bones bleached white,
a closed gate, until they walk to water"?

The moon sleeps in night flowers,
its silence inhabits the hollow dark of bells,
its cool rays build ladders in the grass,
and the tiny horses of the moon
bound free across the waters of the earth,
leap into vapor from dew to ocean
to horizon, and the tiny deer of the moon

graze on the music of crickets...

In the middle of the afternoon I try
to touch the past, but there is nothing
to grab and each hand extended from
those who have walked into memory
offers a coin tarnished with sadness,
or perhaps an autumn leaf skates by
like a letter whose words are faded
from sun– and the absence of everything,
the world gone to the great rages of time,
is motion stilled like a hummingbird
so quick it cannot be captured, its wings
weaving the expanses of sky and earth
while worlds that once seemed urgent
break apart. All the flowing power,
the wealth of the world, falls out of itself
and cannot be caught and yesterday
is so ephemeral it is nothing, an image
made of water hiding in air, images
of yesterday made of evaporation.

All I can do is open my empty hand.

IX

*Walking woods along
the ridge of a river,
I see a ravine where
sun hits grass among
pools of shadow and through
leaves and branches,
slashes of light cut
the ghost-glow air–
and there I recall myself
walking in early years
valleys decades distant,
once at home on earth.*

*It is a long way down
that slide of light!*

*Strange how these passions
never give up!– whose
portal is memory when
innocence was prince
and time seemed eternity.*

But those lands and that

*time were hauled away
when no one was looking
by great sad antiquated
birds, their eyes glazed
like moon on marble,
whose wings thinned
beyond known horizons.*

My home town and all the country I knew
was built on the swash and burble of the Redwood River,
the wide evening discourse of crickets, the solitary coo
of the mourning dove married to the deep emptiness
of clay jars– or their shards scattered among ruins.

And beyond the city limits the clump of dirt flew up!–
on the panicked wings of a shriek to become
a killdeer even as the meadow lark in the fields
whistled golden notes like a flute of sunlight.

Curly dock spiked the ditches with tall declarations
of burnt umber as if scorched by the sun and the corn
stood in strict regiments, its fibrous leaves
rustling with furtive schemes to switch fields
by dark when no one would notice.
                                          And I imagined
my bedroom window journeyed out over the prairie
in the wild night,
                   gathering visions for my sleep
as I listened to the distances talk in the huge

swaying trees,
        hollow syllables,
                vowels of the past...

Ancient graffiti inscribed in stone,
petroglyphs lit by the moon's cold fire,
voices folded into the night wind–

One morning I came awake and saw motes of dust
drift and turn in the rays of the window–
                perhaps
it was dust of disintegrated flowers of another season,
released to the empty spaces–
                or ruins unbuilding
themselves–
        monuments capitals walls reduced
from erosion and lacking intention–
                dust on the sill
and the gravel road beyond town was the dust
of the bread of the ages,
        the eyes of the ages
everywhere dried up and gone and I saw
worlds lost!–
        the dawn of innocent splendors propped
against all the dark of the past as my home town lifted
with the day upon the lethargic gears of work or sharp
cries of birds–
        the wide panorama of the day held
the commotion of arousal: noises and voices,
                bustle

of traffic,
            screech of tires–
                        but also the deep silence
of ancient peoples,
                silence equal and the same in all time,
and then all great words seemed futile,
                            words bold
as water towers with the names of cities against sky,
or anthems, the names of nations, pride and power:
those ages a second or millennium ago–
                            gone–
who but the dead can weep tears of dust into history?

If the last and greatest empire is a sleeping beast
convulsing toward the end of its nightmare of power,
even as its cloud-swaying towers plunged to earth
and its missiles and jet fighters spewed rage!–
                            still:
not all its magnificent balconies of fire built on fire
in foreign cities where the commander's word
sears sky, nor all its weapons, terrible rumblings
or high secret satellites can impress wind or rain
whose rooms always open for the dead– or
the cool ghostly moon whose nacreous soul
pools in the discarded shell by the sea.

What can the power of word or weapon mean
anywhere on earth when the shadow of the planet itself
falls upon nothing in space,
                    falls like nothing falling

through all time–
             and even the cool glow of the moon
haunting its waters means nothing in five billion years
to the sun ripping itself apart?

             Though someone says:
"Let us claim this rock, this cliff above the waves of the sea,
this continent and all its cities and all its time, its fossils
and bones"–
             these mortal bodies, whose senses let us
discover the day,
             come to the day's end, the continent
darkens and no bright knives in the sunset halt the night...

If our cities end as ash falling inside a dusk mirror
and time goes to sleep in the shadows of dates
chiseled in stone, and all the recording angels
of history spin like dust devils grabbing despair
and see only wastelands as if nothing more
had happened, etching fragmented notes on the wind,
but for what purpose?–

             if some squinty lizard-eyed
born-again fascist declares the world his empire
and names it the Apocalypse and ignites the horizons
and as we gaze into tomorrow that has already
forgotten us like a promised land turned to ruins,
the future like a satirical reflection of the past collapsed

into dust and empty as eyes in the skulls of prophets,
some child among us might ask "Who were we?
Was the city also our voice or did we just build walls?"

And perhaps as we fall into history with no one
left to record it, our long story might open all its loss
before us and there would be a clear moment
to wonder, in a collective meditation in the last evening
on earth for our species: did we try to build from
the elements the unfathomable spirit the beauty
of ourselves,
             on those streets where we met ourselves
coming and going and waved farewell the same
as waving hello, the grace of hands a quick flourish
like calligraphy on air that implied an elegant sentence
beyond words–
              and we built our houses from
the laughter and screams of children in the dusk
that floated on the void like the city itself floated–
as though everyone had agreed to dream it?–

or at least, in those cities did we try to locate our yearning
for beauty if its absence was all we could find, or anything
beyond despair?– knowing the place names we invented
shall not keep us in a universe that cares nothing for
names–

or were those cities only places where the powerful

reigned for a little while,
                      and even though
the moonlight haunted our dreams and walked
upon the waters,
                      and even though we were all made
from water,
            they tried to own the waters of the world
to sell to the world as if the hidden hand of the weather
would not touch their hand also and take them away
into the dust with those who thirsted?

Still–
I recall moments in childhood that seemed to locate
in the center of time, when I imagined my voice the echo
of a lineage of all ancestors and nights far back where stars
vastly swirled as they still do in their communal gravities–
and in that deep time the first cricket broke the silence
from the center of its black violin, from the waiting
stillness
a single creak like an immense wheel turning the great
eras
to come–
            and then another note answered,
                            and a third
and soon the night was a wave of pulsing rhythm–
and I imagined the first cricket that spoke in that
distant place called to every cricket since–--
                            and I imagined

someone in some remote evening once skipped a stone
across water,
              which went as far as it could and sank
even as the moon rose,
                    and though I now know stone
locked in itself is gravity and cares nothing for how
or where it falls,
            I know gravity in a poem is grief
that calls back to the first word spoken, these words
I now speak call back and fall through time and silence
to those other skies when I first gazed into the stars,
in that ancient time of my home town where
the lunar-wrapped ghost-child of myself still wanders,
when I felt the earth was enormous dark energy
and I imagined ancestors listening as I listened
in the deep of night for what calls at the center
to be saved when the moon cast its sheen
upon the waters of the earth and upon
the waters of their eyes dreaming as I dreamed
those deep wells where each dawn was born.

    And now I see the moon lift over
    my home town and the wide prairie,
    round and whole with the silence
    of the eons, it lifts then and lifts now:
    in that time when I was there
    and now when I am not.

    And I no longer know the difference
    between time then and time now.

*The moon rises high over horizons
and slides across water, the lakes
and rivers, and the sea where
the dead and the living meet.*

*The moon rides high and the sea
builds and breaks its steps
through our sleep and the moon
flings its light like strange money
upon the shores, rearranging
the dark fates of chaos,*

*and little by little we surrender
all we have gathered by day,
the shimmer of roses that burned
into the dusk, their whorls become
secret vaults of the night,
sleep dissolves the walls
of our bedrooms, and the ground
of our country is nameless,
our shadows join ancestral shadows,
the powers of history we thought
could never be defeated
mean nothing, tanks enter
the quiet fires of rust, we touch
dark waves, the grief of the ages,
everything washed in dream waters,
and with eyes opened by loss,
and with our empty hands,*

we approach the moon...

About the Author

Dale Jacobson's recent books of poetry include *Voices of the Communal Dark* (2000) and *A Walk by the River* (2004), both from Red Dragonfly Press known for its fine hand-printed productions. The latter book is also available in a trade edition. Remarking upon another recent book, his long political poem *Factories and Cities* (2003), the poet Gary David wrote: "*Factories and Cities* is the most powerful long poem I've read in a long time, perhaps since Tom McGrath's *Letter to an Imaginary Friend*. Rooted in a sense of place (the Upper Midwest) and a specific history (the last half of the 20th century), Jacobson's magnum opus speaks to a distant future beyond cynicism, where material equality and universal justice are not just corny, outdated sentiments but an enduring way of life that could well be called sacred." Jacobson has published substantial commentary on the work of Thomas McGrath in *American Poetry Review* and *North Dakota Quarterly*. His close friendship with McGrath led to his providing editorship for the definitive edition of McGrath's epic poem, *Letter to an Imaginary Friend*. In 2005 he was designated Honorary Poet Laureate of North Dakota by the state's Poet Laureate, Larry Woiwode. He teaches in North Dakota and resides in his home state of Minnesota.

NORMANDALE COMMUNITY COLLEGE
LIBRARY
9700 FRANCE AVENUE SOUTH
BLOOMINGTON, MN 55431-4399

Printed in the United States
75512LV00003B/131